Teaching With Favorite
Patricia Polacco Books

BY IMMACULA A. RHODES

SCHOLASTIC
PROFESSIONAL BOOKS

NEW YORK • TORONTO • LONDON • AUCKLAND • SYDNEY
MEXICO CITY • NEW DELHI • HONG KONG • BUENOS AIRES

For José

and Gloria Abeyta...

"Parents are the pride of their children."

(Proverbs 17:6)

Cover illustration from CHICKEN SUNDAY by Patricia Polacco, copyright © 1992 by Babushka, Inc. Used by permission of Philomel Books, an imprint of Penguin Putnam Books for Young Readers, a division of Penguin Putnam Inc.

Cover illustration from THUNDER CAKE by Patricia Polacco, copyright © 1990 by Babushka, Inc. Used by permission of Philomel Books, an imprint of Penguin Putnam Books for Young Readers, a division of Penguin Putnam Inc.

Cover illustration from THE KEEPING QUILT reprinted with the permission of Simon & Schuster Books for Young Readers, an imprint of Simon & Schuster Children's Publishing Division from THE KEEPING QUILT by Patricia Polacco. Copyright © 1988 Patricia Polacco.

Profile of Patricia Polacco from *The Big Book of Picture-Book Authors & Illustrators*, by James Preller (Scholastic Professional Books, 2001). Reprinted by permission of James Preller.

Photo of Patricia Polacco courtesy of Penguin Putnam, © Kenn Klein.

Front cover and interior design by Kathy Massaro
Interior illustrations by Maxie Chambliss, except for page 38 by James Graham Hale

ISBN 0-439-27166-5
Copyright © 2002 by Immacula A. Rhodes
Published by Scholastic Inc.
All rights reserved.
Printed in the U.S.A.

4 5 6 7 8 9 10   40   09 08 07 06 05 04 03

Contents

Books About Patricia Polacco's Personal and Family Experiences

The Fiction, Fantasy, and Folktales of Patricia Polacco

❋ About This Book ❋

The talented and imaginative Patricia Polacco blends her storytelling and artistic skills with perfect precision to create unique children's books. Some of her tales are spun in true-to-life fashion, whereas others assume fantasy or fairy tale qualities. Whatever direction they take, one thing is certain—Polacco's stories inspire readers to appreciate family heritage, examine personal attitudes, and find reason to hope, dream, and reach for the stars. Introduce children to this popular author-illustrator and her works with the creative ideas included in this author study. From exploring curriculum-related topics to examining emotions and family heritage, this book offers a variety of activities to reinforce and extend students' learning with Patricia Polacco books. Following is an overview of the book:

◎ Introducing a Patricia Polacco Author Study

This section includes a collection of ideas to help plan and prepare for your author study. Help children get to know the author with the biographical and personal information in this section, as well as with activities about the author's background.

◎ Teaching Activities for Any Time

Enrich your author study with activities and reproducible activity pages that work well with assorted Polacco titles.

◎ Exploring Books About Patricia Polacco's Personal and Family Experiences

The books in this section focus on traditions and relationships among family members and with the community. Lessons include a story summary, related themes and topics, before- and after-reading discussion ideas, and a wide variety of activities and reproducible activity pages that give children an opportunity to practice curriculum-related skills while learning more about the author and her family.

◎ Exploring the Fiction, Fantasy, and Folktales of Patricia Polacco

Patricia Polacco adds some unexpected twists, a pinch of exaggeration, and a lot of imagination to these enjoyable, unique stories. Use the story-related ideas in this section to reinforce children's learning skills and creativity. Other features include a story summary, related themes and topic, and ready-to-use reproducible activity pages.

◎ More Books by Patricia Polacco

Extend your author study with more Patricia Polacco books. This list includes some of the titles referenced in lessons throughout the book.

◎ Author Study Celebration

Use any or all of these fun activities to conclude your Patricia Polacco author study.

Introducing a Patricia Polacco Author Study

What do your students already know about Patricia Polacco and her books? Let them share their thoughts, then add to what they know with the following story about her childhood memories, her family, and her life as a writer and illustrator.

Meet the Author

Patricia Polacco

Born July 11, 1944, in Lansing, Michigan
Home: Oakland, California

Family Roots

Patricia Polacco grew up listening to the wonderful stories of her parents and grandparents, her head swimming with images and characters. "My fondest memories," she recalls, "are of sitting around a stove or open fire, eating apples and popping corn while listening to the old ones [her grandparents] tell glorious stories about the past."

Patricia was born in Lansing, Michigan. Her parents divorced when she was three years old and her brother, Richard, was seven. Patricia recalls, "Even though my parents lived apart, they both were very involved in our lives. We spent the school year with my mother and her parents on a small farm in Union City, Michigan, and the summers with my father in Williamston, Michigan."

In Patricia Polacco's books, as in her life, family roots are important. The old ones provided most of the inspiration for her stories. Patricia says, "Babushka [Grandma] and her family came from the Ukraine, just outside of Kiev in Russia. My Diadushka [Granpa] came from Soviet Georgia. My mother's parents were great historians, but they also took us to the world of fancy and magic with stories. People on both sides of my family saw perfectly ordinary events as miraculous. And without this appreciation of even the smallest, tenderest little thing, you're doomed."

(continued on next page)

As a writer and illustrator, Patricia brings this same sense of appreciation to her books. She's as comfortable weaving a colorful yarn based on her Russian heritage as she is retelling an event from her childhood. Her stories are rich in cultural detail and filled with characters of different ages, races, and religions. And always there is a deep pleasure in the simplest things. "You have to look for the miracles in very ordinary events," insists Patricia.

At the age of seven, Patricia moved with her mother to Oakland, California, and returned to Michigan each summer to spend time with her father. Filled with a diverse array of people, Oakland was an exciting place for young Patricia. She still lives there. With obvious pride, Patricia describes her neighborhood: "We live in an urban mixed neighborhood, which means that my neighbors come in as many colors, ideas, and belief systems as there are people on this planet."

Patricia derives great satisfaction from seeing different cultures come together in mutual understanding. "Instead of separating and pulling apart, we should be uniting and pulling together," she says. This theme is sounded again and again in her stories.

Profile of Patricia Polacco from *The Big Book of Picture-Book Authors & Illustrators*, by James Preller (Scholastic Professional Books, 2001). Reprinted by permission of James Preller. Photo of Patricia Polacco courtesy of Penguin Putnam, © Kenn Klein.

Correlations to the Language Arts Standards

The activities in this book are designed to support you in meeting the following standards outlined by the Mid-Continent Regional Educational Laboratory (MCREL), an organization that collects and synthesizes national and state K–12 curriculum standards.

Uses the general skills and strategies of the reading process:

- Understands how print is organized and read
- Creates mental images from pictures and print
- Uses meaning clues to aid comprehension and make predictions about content

Uses reading skills and strategies to understand and interpret a variety of literary texts:

- Uses reading skills and strategies to understand a variety of familiar literary passages and texts, including fiction
- Knows main ideas or theme, setting, main characters, main events, sequence, and problems in stories
- Makes simple inferences regarding the order of events and possible outcomes
- Relates stories to personal experiences

Uses the general skills and strategies of the writing process:

- Uses writing and other methods to describe familiar persons, places, objects, or experiences
- Writes in a variety of forms or genres, including responses to literature

Source: A Compendium of Standards and Benchmarks for K–12 Education (Mid-Continent Regional Educational Laboratory, 1995)

Learn More!

Patricia Polacco writes children's books straight from the heart of her own experience and those of her family. And, based on the stories inspired by her background, family heritage, and the diverse influences in her life, Polacco has certainly enjoyed an interesting life! Use the following activities to reinforce cross-curricular skills while students learn more about this unique author-illustrator.

- List information learned about the author from pages 5–6. Add to the list as students learn more about Polacco during the author study, including information they gather from book covers and jackets, book introductions, stories about her personal experiences, her Web site, and her autobiography, *Firetalking* (from the Meet the Author series by Richard C. Owen Publishers, Inc.).

- Help children locate and mark on a globe (or world map) the different places in which the author has lived and studied.

- As children discover the places from which Polacco's relatives originate—such as Ukraine, Republic of Georgia, and Ireland—help them locate the corresponding countries on a globe or world map.

- Help students create a family tree of Polacco's relatives, using information from her books. As you read her family-based stories, ask children to locate on the tree the family member that corresponds to each character.

- Have children list events in the stories that are based on Polacco's own experiences.

- Chart each book title, the person or people to whom it is dedicated, and the book characters. Then ask children to determine whether the dedication might be connected to the story in some way. Have them discuss their ideas. On the chart, invite children to check off all the characters that are or were drawn from Polacco's life. Discuss the relationship of each to the author.

- To demonstrate Polacco's unique style of developing stories, encourage students to sit in rocking chairs for quiet blocks of time and recall their own special experiences. They can write about their ideas and create Polacco-style drawings to go with them.

❖ Story ❖
Connections

Polacco compares herself to Appelemando in *Appelemando's Dreams*: When a story is "boiling" in her head, her thoughts and images take flight and float up above her. Ask children to "cook up" stories in their heads. Have them illustrate different scenes from their stories on cloud cutouts, then help them string their sequenced drawings together. Invite students to share their stories with the class. Afterward, suspend the drawings from the ceiling so that the stories float above children's heads.

Polacco's family experiences have inspired ideas for many of her stories. Group together the stories inspired by her family. Then sort the books by their source of inspiration: from her mother's or father's side of the family. Compare and contrast the influence of each set of relatives on Polacco's stories.

Teaching Activities for Any Time

Enhance, extend, and enlighten students' learning with this collection of ideas that work well with any of Patricia Polacco's books.

A Keeping Quilt of Books

Have your class create a "keeping quilt" of Polacco's family of books. As you share each book, invite a pair of children to decorate a paper square to represent the story. Arrange the squares in quilt fashion on a length of bulletin board paper.

Book of Knowledge (Language Arts/Social Studies)

Polacco's great-grandfather promoted reading by encouraging her mother to chase knowledge through the pages of a book. In keeping with this advice, create a class "Book of Knowledge." Have children use the book to record (and illustrate) new vocabulary and information about different cultures and traditions from Polacco's books. Be sure to include references to each book in which the information occurs. Later, encourage students to use the class book as a resource for exploring personal interests as well as for researching different cultures.

Fact or Fiction (Language Arts)

Challenge children to sort a group of Polacco's books by fact and fiction. Help students search each book's jacket, summary, dedication line, introduction, and author information to determine which category it best fits. After categorizing the books, have children discuss how and why they arrived at their decisions for each book. To extend this activity for Polacco's fact-based fiction, encourage students to sort the realistic from the fictitious events.

A Treasury of Books (Art)

In *Aunt Chip and the Great Triple Creek Dam Affair*, Aunt Chip told her nephew that "books are a treasure." Patricia Polacco's books are most especially books to be treasured. Ask children to illustrate half-sheets of paper to represent their favorite Polacco stories. Have them label each picture with the corresponding book title. Give children copies of the treasure chest booklet cover on page 13, then have them follow these steps to assemble their books.

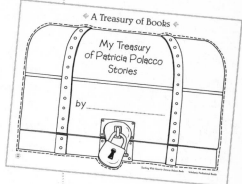

- Color and cut out the treasure chest pattern.

- Staple story pages between the cover and a sheet of matching construction paper.

- Trim the edges of the pages to match the shape of the booklet cover.

That's Incredible! (Language Arts)

Polacco describes several incredible events in her books, including a meteor landing in her yard, animals decorating a tree, a doll that comes to life, a goose that lays decorated eggs, a magical rock, a boy who migrates with a flock of geese, and a wren with mystical powers. Remind children of some of these events. Then invite them to pretend they are journalists in search of the story behind one of these events. Encourage students to use the actual stories as well as input from other imaginative students to gather information for their own stories. Then have them tell their incredible stories in incredible ways, such as in newspaper articles, tape-recorded "broadcasts," or in a class-designed "Incredible Tales!" magazine.

Story Time Lines (Language Arts)

Have groups of children create story time lines by drawing different scenes from Polacco's books on white paper plates. Label the plates (on the back) to show the sequence. Affix magnetic tape to the back of each plate, then challenge children to sequence the story plates on a magnetic surface. After they check their work, have students use the picture plates to retell the story.

✦ Story ✦ Connections

A meteor really did land in Polacco's grandmother's yard. The meteor is now the family headstone in a cemetery not far from its original landing spot. Ask students to share their ideas about what they would do with their own personal meteors.

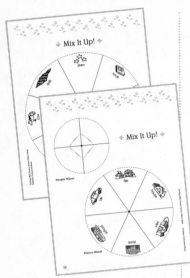

Mix It Up! (Language Arts/Art)

Invite children to create amusing mixed-up stories with a story wheel. Give each student a copy of the wheel patterns on pages 14 and 15. Ask children to draw the following in each quarter of the people wheel: a self-portrait, a sibling or friend, a parent or caregiver, a picture of a grandparent or other relative. Have them color and cut out all the wheels, and stack them by size, with the largest on the bottom. Next, help students attach the wheels to a paper plate with a brass fastener. Finally, instruct 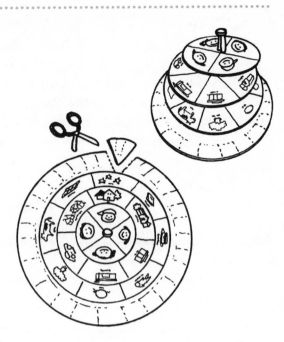 them to notch the plate rim, as shown above. To use, children align one picture on each wheel with the notch. Then they make up an incredible tale involving the object, place, and person designated on the story wheel.

Terrific Traditions (Social Studies)

Help students list some of the family traditions that Polacco weaves into her stories. Then invite children to tell about their own special family traditions. As a follow-up activity, plan a tradition day on which children and family members show and tell about their special family traditions.

The Young and Young at Heart (Language Arts)

Many of Polacco's stories focus on relationships between young and elderly characters. Discuss some of these relationships with children. Then have children imagine that they are the young characters in Polacco's stories. Have them write about their relationships with the elderly story characters. To extend this idea, ask students to tell about their relationships with elderly family members or friends. Invite them to create "Hello!" or "Thank You!" cards for these special folks.

Sibling Matters (Language Arts)

The author and her brother appear in several Polacco books, such as *My Rotten Redheaded Older Brother*, *My Ol' Man*, and *The Trees of the Dancing Goats*. After reading these stories, discuss the relationship between young Patricia and Richard. Then ask children to share stories about their own sibling relationships. Have them construct booklets about these personal relationships, with each page showing the siblings engaged in different kinds of activities or interactions. Invite children who do not have siblings to draw pictures of imaginary interactions or to illustrate the activities and interactions between Patricia and Richard.

Special Times With Relatives (Social Studies/Art)

In several of Polacco's stories, the young characters visit their relatives during vacations and special holidays. Invite children to tell about their special visits with relatives. If students know the states (or countries) of their relatives' homes, help them locate these places on a globe or world map. Then have your class create a mural filled with illustrations of their experiences.

Expressive Emotions (Social Studies/Drama)

Polacco's art depicts very expressive characters. After reading one of her books, such as *My Rotten Redheaded Older Brother*, review the illustrations and list the different expressions represented by the characters. Then randomly point to different characters in the book and have children name and imitate each character's expression.

✣ Story ✣
Connections

Patricia Polacco's relationship with her grandparents has had a tremendous influence on her life. This is reflected in her many stories in which young characters interact with elderly persons. Discuss these relationships with your class. Invite children to name some ways in which the child and adult characters influence each other.

In the indoor scenes of some of her books, Polacco displays "framed" black-and-white photos. The photos are usually pictures of people that appear in the books. Invite children to find and identify some of the photographed people in *Chicken Sunday*, *My Rotten Redheaded Older Brother*, and *Aunt Chip and the Great Triple Creek Dam Affair*.

Mystery Characters (Language Arts)

Ask children to write first-person descriptions of Polacco's characters and their experiences. Then have students sign their character names on their papers. Put the descriptions in a paper bag. During group time, pull out and read one paper at a time. Challenge children to guess the identity of each character.

Character Posters (Language Arts/Art)

Help children learn more about the characters in Polacco's stories with this activity. First, ask student pairs to choose characters of interest to them. Then have the pairs search the appropriate books to learn as much as possible about their selected characters. Next, have children create picture posters for their characters, labeling the posters with bits of information about their characters. Finally, invite children to share their posters with the class. Later, display the posters for other classes and visitors to enjoy.

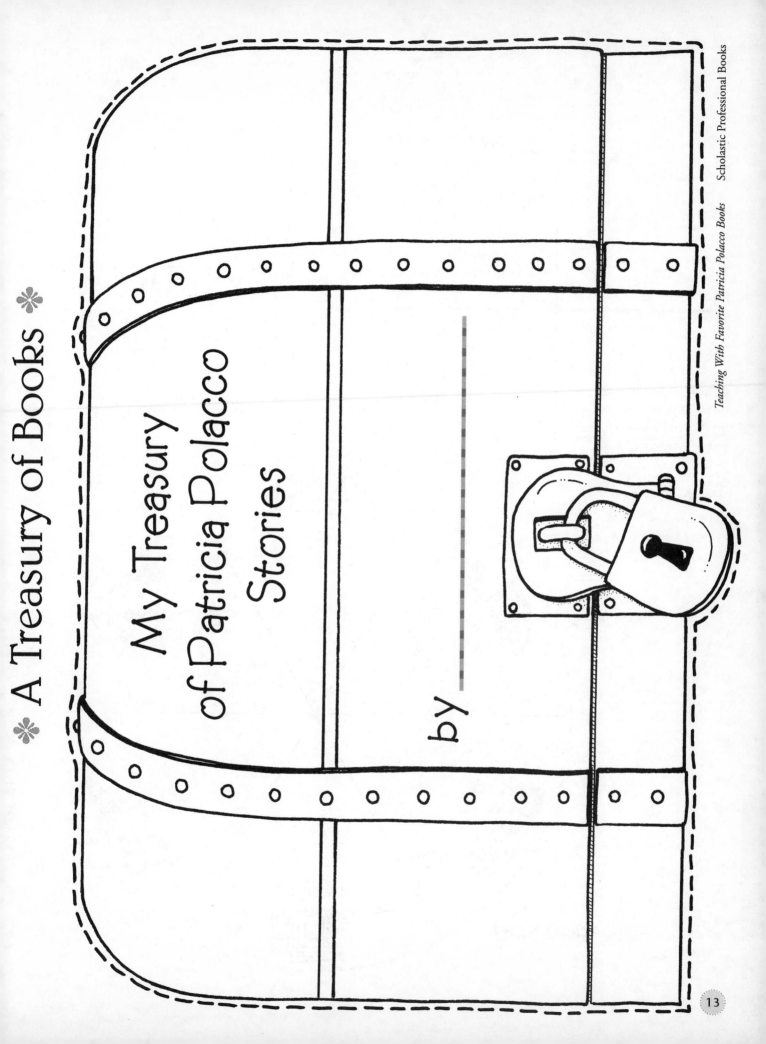

※ A Treasury of Books ※

My Treasury
of Patricia Polacco
Stories

by _____

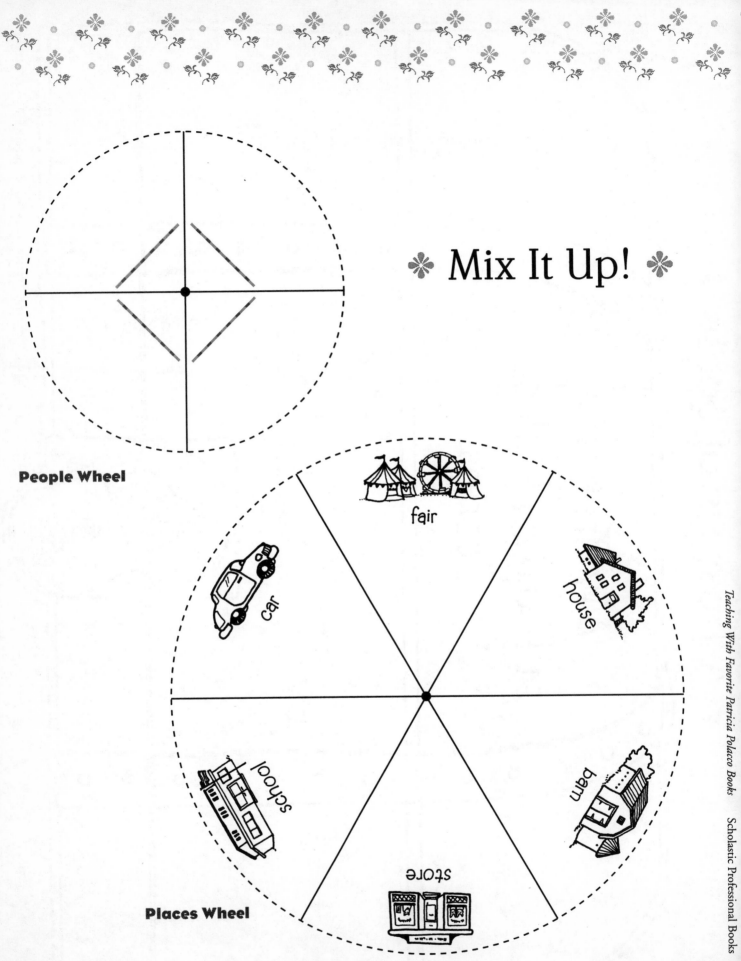

❋ Mix It Up! ❋

People Wheel

Places Wheel

Teaching With Favorite Patricia Polacco Books   Scholastic Professional Books

❋ Mix It Up! ❋

stars

book

quilt

cake

cow

meteorite

tree

egg

Objects Wheel

The Keeping Quilt

(SIMON & SCHUSTER, 1988)

A beloved quilt, made from old clothes, symbolizes the author's family heritage as mothers pass it to daughters over several generations. Throughout the years, the quilt witnesses many special occasions—Sabbath observances, birthdays, engagements, and weddings. And so the tradition continues as the author anticipates the day she passes the quilt to her own daughter.

Related Themes and Topics

▲▲▲▲▲▲

❋ Quilts

❋ Family traditions/ heritage

❋ Special events

❋ Passage of time

Before Reading

Show children the quilt on the book cover. If desired, also display a real quilt made of various fabrics. Then poll students to find out how many have special quilts in their families. Afterward, ask them to share their thoughts about what a "keeping quilt" is and what makes it special.

After Reading

The keeping quilt was special indeed, for it witnessed many memorable events in the author's family. Ask students to list the different occasions in which the quilt was included and the family members who were present. Then invite children to share their personal stories about quilts or other special items that have been passed among family members. Later, invite students (and their families) to bring in their special items to share with the class.

Class Family Quilt (Social Studies/Art)

Help students create this special quilt to represent each member of your class "family." To begin, use a permanent marker to section a flat white sheet into enough squares to equal or exceed the number of class members, including yourself. Ask children to bring in from home their favorite things made from cloth—such as articles of clothing, blankets, or patterned stuffed animals. Invite children to use fabric markers and various craft materials to reproduce the patterns from the fabric onto the sheet squares. Be sure to copy your own favorite pattern onto the quilt, too. When the quilt is completed, ask children, one at a time, to show and tell about the actual objects. After each child's turn, have students find the quilt square that corresponds to that child's object. Display the quilt and send the objects back home with children.

Quilt Dance (Movement)

Dancing was a big part of many of the celebrations that included the keeping quilt. Have children identify the celebrations in the story at which dancing took place. Then invite them to involve their class quilt in a special celebration—a quilt dance! To prepare, drape the quilt over a table. Then encourage students to creatively move around the quilt as you play musical selections representing different cultures, especially those of your students.

If Quilts Could Talk (Language Arts/Social Studies)

If quilts could talk, what would your students' personal quilts say? Find out with this project. Show children how to fold sheets of construction paper into six-section grids. Ask them to cut out rectangles of decorative gift wrap to fit the sections. Then have them glue one edge of a rectangle to each section, creating quilts with flaps. When the glue dries, ask children to lift the flaps and write messages about special occasions in their lives. During group time, invite students, one at a time, to read the messages under their quilt flaps. You'll find that these special quilts have lots to say about your students!

Tip

▲▲▲▲▲

Just as the keeping quilt was a special guest at many family events, include your class quilt as an honored guest at special class events. You might use the quilt to cover a table for a birthday celebration, or as a special prop for a dramatic production. For another use, let the quilt serve as a robe for children to wear for special presentations.

Story Connections

Patricia Polacco loves to include real people from her life in her stories. For example, the African-American man at her wedding in *The Keeping Quilt* is Stewart Washington, one of her real-life best friends! Tell children that Stewart is a main character in another story that also features Polacco as herself. Then give students a stack of Polacco books and challenge them to find the story that features both characters (*Chicken Sunday*).

End-of-Year Quilt Canopy
(Social Studies)

The keeping quilt was included in many life passages in the story. Use your class quilt as part of an end-of-year celebration to represent students' passage to their next grade level. To prepare, make a scroll and bookmark for each child. (See patterns on pages 19 and 20.) Complete a scroll for each child, and tie it up with colorful ribbon. Place each scroll in a small bag, along with a small silk flower, a treat (such as fruit snacks or trail mix), and the bookmark, to represent your wish for a life filled with love (the flower), flavor (the treat), and knowledge (the bookmark). Then set up your class quilt as a canopy. During the celebration, invite children to pass under the quilt canopy one at a time to receive their "diplomas" (or other end-of-year documents) and special wish-filled goody bags.

(Name)

_M_ay your life

be filled with love, flavor,

and knowledge.

(Date) _(Teacher)_

My Favorite Books
by Patricia Polacco

"**Books are a treasure.**"

—Aunt Chip,
from *Aunt Chip*
and the Great Triple Creek
Dam Affair
by Patricia Polacco

(Name)

My Ol' Man

(PENGUIN PUTNAM, 1995)

Bursting with enthusiasm and eyes sparkling, Bill Barber tells his family about his discovery at Potter's Pond—a huge rock with mysterious markings. Not just any old rock, but a magic rock! After losing his job a few days later, Bill works odd jobs to make ends meet, tries to sell his beloved cruiser, and makes daily visits to the special rock. Finally, Bill's luck changes and incredible things happen: He gets an unexpected job offer, the magic rock mysteriously disappears, and the Barber family learns the true source of magic!

Related Themes and Topics

▲▲▲▲▲

❋ Family

❋ Perseverance

❋ Positive thinking

❋ Feelings

Before Reading

Ask for a show of hands to find out how many students enjoy taking trips. Then invite them to tell about things they enjoy doing while traveling. Do any of your students collect stories while on the road? After your discussion, read *My Ol' Man* aloud to introduce children to the traveling salesman, Bill Barber—a story collector, "dream keeper," and "wish keeper."

After Reading

Discussion Starters

Bill Barber had contrasting feelings about his discovery of the rock and losing his job. Ask children to discuss his feelings about both events. Then label one side of a chart with descriptive words for his feelings about the rock (such as *happy* and *hopeful*) and the other side with words describing his feelings about the loss of his job (such as *sad, upset,* and *sorry*). Invite students to list things on each side that cause them to have similar feelings.

Tip

▲▲▲▲▲

Encourage students to use their stories for the Magic Microphone activity on page 23.

Cruisin' and Collecting Tales (Language Arts/Social Studies)

Ask children to help decorate a large appliance box to resemble the old cruiser in the story. Stock the car with comfortable pillows, clipboards, and various writing implements. Then invite students to take pretend journeys in the

cruiser, using their imagination to collect stories as they travel. Have them write and illustrate their stories to later share with the class. To extend this activity, you might suggest a state, country, or a specific location—such as a fire station or zoo—for children to "visit."

Telling Tales (Language Arts)

In the book, storyteller Bill Barber became a radio announcer. Set up a center with a tape recorder to represent a radio booth. Then invite children to broadcast their stories from Cruisin' and Collecting Tales (above) into the tape player. Or have them create and tell new stories over the radio. Play the recordings for the class to enjoy.

✤ Story ✤ Connections

Patricia Polacco tells several stories that involve magical or mysterious happenings. Help children identify some of these stories. (*Babushka's Doll, Rechenka's Eggs,* and *Meteor!* are a few.) Discuss the "magic" that happens in each story.

Secret Rock Messages (Language Arts/Art)

The Barbers' magic rock had lots of old mysterious lines. In Patricia's painting on the last page, the lines on the rock appear to be symbols, possibly from an ancient culture. Explain that long ago, symbols were used to communicate thoughts and events. Help your class create a set of symbols and meanings for the symbols. Then ask children to cut out brown construction-paper rocks and label them with messages, using the class-generated symbols. Challenge students to "read" their classmates' mysterious messages.

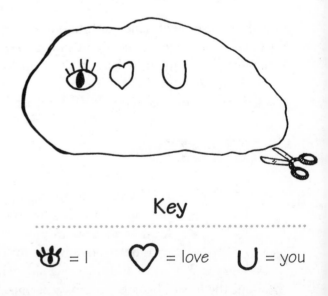

Key

👁 = I   ♡ = love   U = you

Magic Microphone (Language Arts)

Invite children to help make special microphones to "broadcast" their own versions of this story and other magical Polacco tales (see Story Connections, page 22) as well as their own story creations. To begin, cut a three-inch polystyrene ball in half. Paint one of the halves black. After the paint dries, glue the black dome onto the lid of a tall canister. Cover the canister with black or silver paper and snap on the domed lid. It's time to go on the air!

Tip
▲▲▲▲▲

Children can roll up their stories and place them inside the microphone canister. During group time, remove one paper at a time from the microphone. Invite the author to tell the story, using the microphone.

Someone Special (Language Arts/Art)

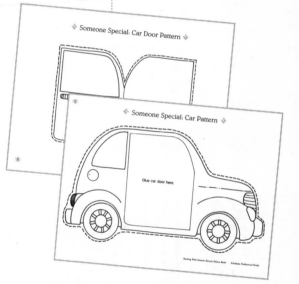

Patricia and Ritchie knew that they had a special dad. After discussing the qualities that made Bill Barber so special, invite students to make these neat cruisers to share about someone special to them. Have children cut out the car and door patterns (pages 24 and 25). Ask them to write about someone special on the back of the door cutout. Have children fold their car doors where indicated and then illustrate their special person in the door window. Instruct them to color their cars and doors and glue the door to the car. Encourage students to share their creations with their families.

Someone Special: Car Pattern

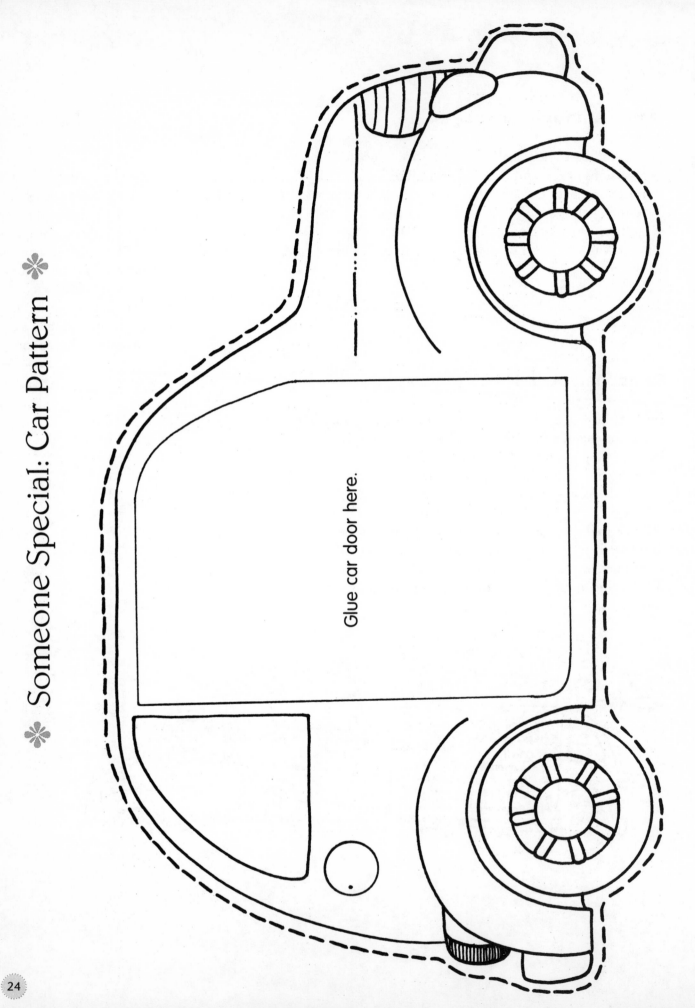

Glue car door here.

Teaching With Favorite Patricia Polacco Books   Scholastic Professional Books

✳ Someone Special: Car Door Pattern ✳

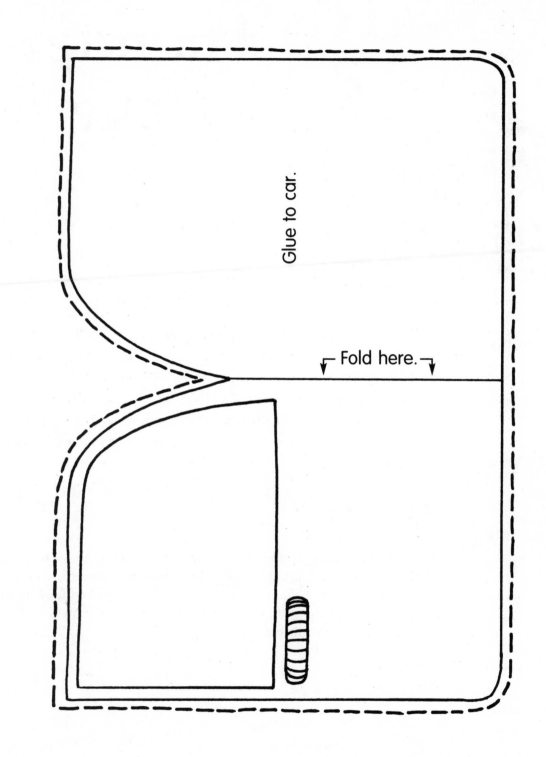

Glue to car.

⌐ Fold here. ⌐

Teaching With Favorite Patricia Polacco Books   Scholastic Professional Books

Thunder Cake

(PHILOMEL BOOKS, 1990)

Related Themes and Topics

▲▲▲▲▲

❋ Family life

❋ Fear

❋ Counting

❋ Cooking

When it begins to thunder, young Patricia fearfully dives under the bed. To coax her out, Grandma solicits her granddaughter's help to make a thunder cake—a cake that must be mixed and in the oven before the storm arrives. With the storm fast approaching, the two hurriedly gather and mix the ingredients. And when the cake makes it to the oven in time, Patricia discovers that she has conquered her fear of thunder—as well as a few more fears along the way!

Before Reading

What do your students fear? Name a few common childhood fears, such as darkness, sleeping alone, getting lost, and thunderstorms. (Be sure to include any fears that are specific to your students.) Invite children to share their experiences in dealing with the fearful situation. Brainstorm positive ways to deal with and overcome each fear.

After Reading

Have children list each instance of fear experienced by the girl in the story, such as her fear of thunder, Nellie Peck Hen, Kick Cow, the walk through Tangleweed Woods, and entering the dark shed. Have them describe how she responded to each situation. Was she afraid? Brave? How did she overcome her fear in each situation?

Thunder-Cake Time Lines (Language Arts/Math)

Help children visually follow the events of this story by making thunder-cake time lines. Give groups of children a length of bulletin board paper. Ask children to draw a line across the paper to divide it in half lengthwise. Above the line, have students label the sequence of the storm, starting at the point when the storm is 10 miles away. Below the line, have them label the girl's activity corresponding to each storm event. Let students illustrate their time lines, then use them to retell the story.

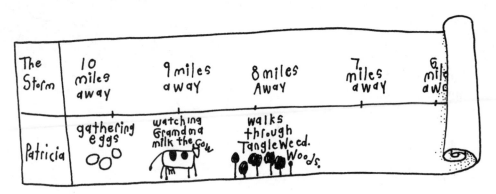

Secret Ingredients (Science/Math)

Babushka's cake had a secret ingredient—tomatoes. Explain that a tomato is really a fruit, although it is often thought of as a vegetable. Ask children to name other "secret" fruits that might be used in a cake recipe. List student responses on a chart. Then have children initial the columns labeled with their favorite fruits. Count and compare the results in each column to discover which fruit is the class favorite. If desired, invite children to bring in their favorite fresh fruit for snack. Have them compare the various fruits. How are they alike? How are they different? Then encourage students to explore the fruits with their senses. Ask them to describe the sensations they experience from the fruit, using words such as *round, soft, sweet,* and *crunchy.*

Stir Up a Storm (Drama)

Invite small groups to creatively stir up pretend thunderstorms using flashlights, various instruments, classroom materials, and their own creative resources (such as tapping the patter of rain with their feet). Then invite one group at a time to showcase its storm. Challenge children to judge the closeness of the storm by measuring the interval between the lightning flashes and thunderclaps.

✦ Story ✦
Connections

Patricia Polacco uses several different names for her grandparents: Grandma, Babushka, Grampa, and Diadushka. Invite students to share the special names they call their grandparents— and why they use these names.

Thunder-Cake Math (Math)

Cook up some sweet math skills with these individual Thunder Cakes. Give each child a copy of page 29. Have children color and cut out the pattern pieces, then guide them in following these steps to put the cake together.

◎ Color and cut out the cake patterns.

◎ Cut out the sections where indicated on the cake.

◎ Glue a strawberry over each cutout section, as shown.

◎ Glue a stem behind each dot on the number wheel.

◎ Attach the wheel to the cake with a brass fastener.

Place plastic strawberries in your math center. To practice numeral recognition and/or addition facts, have children turn their wheels so that a stem rests above each strawberry. Have them lift the strawberry flaps, identify each numeral, and count out the corresponding number of strawberries. Or have them add the numerals, using the strawberry counters as needed.

Bravery Banners (Language Arts/Social Studies)

Although the girl did not feel brave, just look at all of her brave actions! After discussing her courageous acts, invite children to brainstorm words or expressions that relate to bravery—for example, *fearless, courageous, confident,* and *lion-hearted.* Have children make bravery banners to showcase their bravery. Give children bulletin board paper cut into large banner flag shapes. Ask them to write words or expressions and draw pictures on their banners that tell about their own acts of bravery.

✦ Story ✦
Connections

Let students help prepare the thunder-cake recipe in the back of the book. (Check for food allergies before serving.) While students enjoy their treat, ask them to recall which ingredients came from farm animals. Revisit illustrations of the farm animals in this book and other Polacco books, such as *My Rotten Redheaded Older Brother, Meteor!,* and *The Bee Tree*. Then tell students that Patricia Polacco's childhood farm experiences influence her animal illustrations. Students might like to try their hands at drawing expressive Polacco-style animals.

✻ Thunder-Cake Math ✻

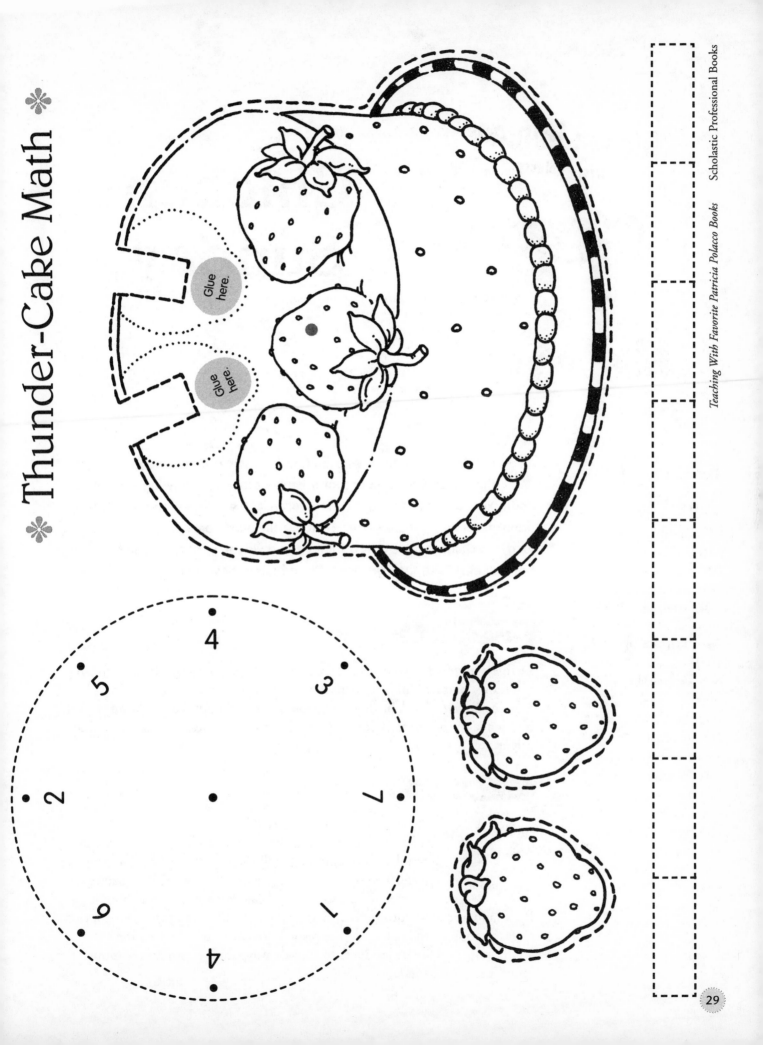

Glue here.

Glue here.

2

5

4

6

4

7

3

1

Teaching With Favorite Patricia Polacco Books   Scholastic Professional Books

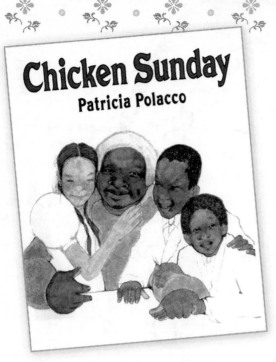

Chicken Sunday

(PENGUIN PUTNAM, 1995)

Related Themes and Topics

▲▲▲▲▲

❋ Family life

❋ Conflict resolution

❋ Responsibility

❋ Friendship

Patricia, Stewart, and Winston find themselves in the wrong place at the wrong time, and are mistakenly accused of throwing eggs at Mr. Kodinski's hat shop. To prove their innocence, the children give Mr. Kodinski hand-decorated pysanky eggs—just like the ones from his homeland. Before long, the children have a new friend and a way to earn money to buy the hat that Miss Eula, their gramma, has admired for so long.

Before Reading

Define *tradition* for your class. Share some of your own family or friendship traditions, and let children share theirs. Then show students the cover of *Chicken Sunday*. Explain that this book mentions a Sunday tradition shared by friends in the story. Before reading, let students guess what that tradition might be.

After Reading

Explain to children that the eggs in this story were used to symbolize good and bad. Tell them that the expressions *good egg* and *bad egg* are sometimes used to describe a person's character. To illustrate, label one large egg cutout "Good Eggs" and a second cutout "Bad Eggs." Have students contrast the behavior of each group in the story and the results. Record their ideas on the appropriate egg. Invite students to suggest ways their classmates demonstrate "good egg" behaviors.

Egg Examinations (Science)

How familiar are your children with eggs? To find out, bring in several raw eggs for them to examine. Have them feel the smooth outer shell and note its oval shape. Then carefully crack open an egg, noting its thin, fragile shell. Empty the contents into a bowl and have children compare the yellow yolk to the clear egg white. Pierce the yolk with a fork. What happens? To further the egg investigation, cook some eggs in different ways—boiled, fried, and scrambled. Can children identify the different parts of the cooked eggs? What happened to the clear part of the eggs when they were cooked? Invite children to taste the different egg preparations to determine which is their favorite.

Tip

▲▲▲▲▲

Check for food allergies before letting children sample the eggs. Have children wash their hands after handling the raw eggs.

Egg-Throw Extravaganza (Math)

For a math activity that really measures up, try this egg-toss game. In an open grassy area, create a large egg shape using a piece of yarn. Ask children, one at a time, to stand at a marked distance from the yarn egg and throw a plastic egg into it. Have children use a length of yarn to measure the distance they tossed the egg. Back in the classroom, have children help each other to measure their yarn lengths with a measuring tape or yardstick. Record each child's measurement on an egg cutout. Have children sequence their eggs by the distance labeled on them. Use the eggs to make up math problems—for example, "Which three egg throws were the closest in distance?" or "How many egg throws were between [number] and [number] feet?"

Eggs by the Dozen (Math)

In the story, the children decorated almost a dozen pysanky eggs. Do children know how many items are in a dozen? After taking their guesses, show them an egg carton. Explain that it holds one dozen—or 12—eggs. Place the egg carton in your math center with other egg cartons, egg cutouts, and a large supply of plastic eggs (or any other type of counter). Challenge children to fill each carton with eggs, close it, and set it aside. Have them take one paper egg for each dozen they fill. How many dozens of eggs are in the center?

Tip

▲▲▲▲▲

To extend this activity, students can total the number of individual eggs in the cartons by counting or figuring on paper.

Culture Courses (Social Studies)

Chicken Sunday features characters from different cultures who share with and learn about each other. Invite family members or guests representing different cultures to share information about their culture and traditions with your class. If possible, have them demonstrate or teach a craft or art technique that is unique to their culture.

Thank-You Cards (Language Arts/Art)

Spaseeba was Mr. Kodinski's Russian word for *thank you.* Invite children to make these special thank-you cards to express their appreciation to a family member, friend, or teacher. First, have students fold construction paper in half to make a card. Have them write *Spaseeba!* on the front of their cards, then add bold, colorful Polacco-style designs. Ask children to write their message of thanks on the inside, then deliver their cards along with a heartfelt verbal *spaseeba.* For more fun with language, challenge children to use this word in place of *thank you* for an entire school day!

Paper Pysanky Eggs (Art)

Ask children to observe the intricate designs of the decorated eggs in the book. Then invite them to create these semi-glossy pysanky eggs from paper egg cutouts. Give children copies of the egg patterns on page 34. Have students use colored pencils to make patterns on the eggs, then paint their eggs with a watercolor wash. While their eggs dry, mix white glue with water (to a thin consistency). Have children apply two coats of the glue mixture to their eggs, letting them dry between each application.

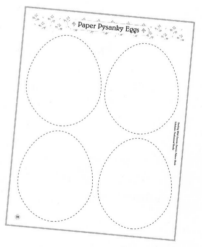

Hats Galore! Store (Math/Social Studies)

For the perfect hat and so much more, send your students to Hats Galore! A visit to this little hat shop will build a range of skills—from working with money to becoming smart consumers. Gather a collection of hats or have children create hats from craft materials. Have children help price the hats, arrange them in a display, and post a shop sign ("Hats Galore!"). Stock the shop with play money, purses, wallets, mirrors, sales receipt pads, and a cash register. (If desired, children might also price and "sell" their decorated eggs from Paper Pysanky Eggs, page 32.) Let children take turns playing shoppers and store clerks.

Hats Galore

✦ Story ✦
Connections

Patricia Polacco uses words from different languages in many of her books. To help children associate these words with their English counterparts, cut out an egg shape for each word. (You can use the patterns on page 34.) Label the top of the egg with the foreign-language word and the bottom with the corresponding English word. Cut each egg into a two-piece puzzle. (Be sure to make each puzzle slightly different.) Invite children to match up the words by putting the puzzles together.

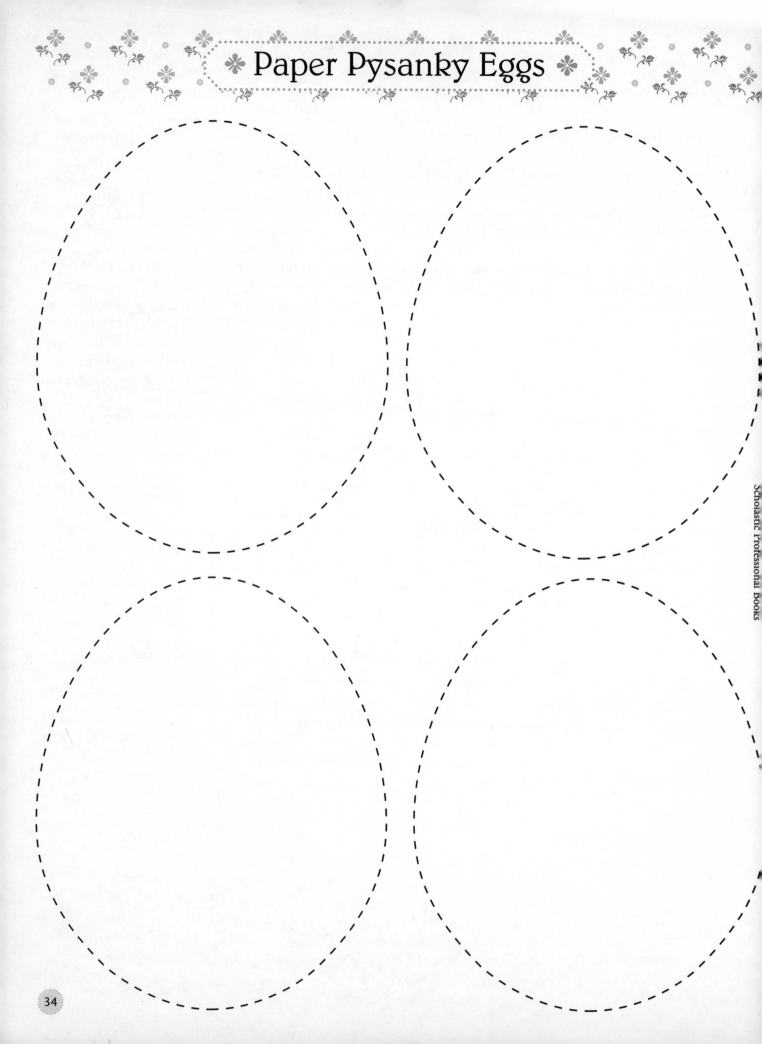

My Rotten Redheaded Older Brother

(PENGUIN PUTNAM, 1995)

Richard could run faster, climb higher, and burp louder than his younger sister, Patricia. In fact, he could do everything better—and he loved to tease her about it! That's why frustrated Patricia made a "shooting star" wish that she could do something—anything—better than Richard. But when her wish comes true, the two children discover that love overpowers sibling rivalry in times of crisis.

Before Reading

Poll students to find out which ones have older siblings—brothers or sisters. Do any of them have siblings who are four years older? Invite children to describe their relationships with their older siblings. Be sure to share your personal experiences if you also have older siblings. Then show students the book cover. Ask them to comment on how they think the pictured brother and sister might relate to each other.

After Reading

Young Patricia marveled that her "Bubbie" could love her rotten, redheaded, older brother. Remind children that their families love them, even when they may not be on their best behavior. Encourage students to share their personal experiences about some of these times. To help students

Related Themes and Topics

▲▲▲▲▲

❊ Family life

❊ Sibling rivalry

❊ Self-concept

appreciate this unconditional love, invite them to create some simple foldout reminders. First, have children accordion-fold a strip of paper. Have them glue a heart on the top section. Then have children complete the following sentence on each additional section: My _____ loves me even when I _____ . Encourage children to share these reminders with those who love them.

"Wish Upon a Star" Booklets (Language Arts)

Patricia made a wish upon a shooting star, and your students can, too! Invite each child to trace and cut out several large identical stars, then write about and illustrate his or her wishes on the stars. Have children make a cover for their booklets by dabbing glue on an extra star and sprinkling it with glitter. Help children stack their star pages, then place the cover on top and staple at two points. Invite children to share their booklets with the class.

To create a display with the booklets, cover a bulletin board with dark blue paper. Glue strips of Velcro® around the display (one per child), and to the back of each booklet. Invite children to place their booklets on the display, then use a gold glitter pen to draw star streaks directly on the background, so that their booklets resemble shooting stars. During reading time, encourage children to include these booklets in their reading choices. Children can easily remove a booklet, read it, and then carefully return it to its place on the display.

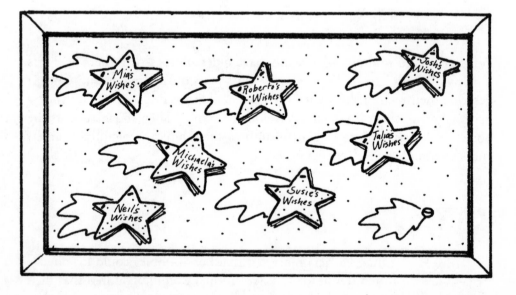

✦ Story ✦ Connections

Patricia Polacco shows real photos of herself and her family on the inside cover of this book as well as in *My Ol' Man*. She also uses photos to illustrate some of her other books. Share these photos with the class. Then designate a bulletin board as a class photo album page. Invite children to display individual and family pictures to share with the class. Let children make triangle-shaped photo corners from construction paper to put around their photographs.

Merry-Go-Round Mobiles (Social Studies/Language Arts)

This unique merry-go-round will give children an opportunity to acquaint classmates with their family members. Have students follow the directions below to make the merry-go-round. Then invite them to share their creations with the class before taking them home.

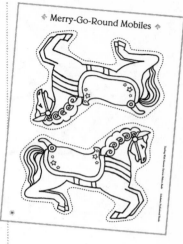

◎ Decorate the bottom of a 9-inch paper plate to represent a carousel roof. Make two holes near the center of the plate.

◎ Staple the ends of a colored sentence strip together to create a ring.

◎ Color and cut out up to four carousel horses (page 38). Have children write a family member's name on each horse's saddle.

◎ Glue a wide craft stick to the back of each horse. Glue the horses to the ring, as shown.

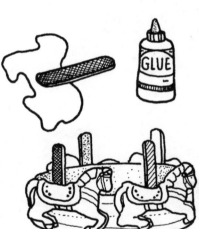

◎ Put glue on the unattached end of each craft stick. Carefully press the roof onto the sticks.

◎ After the glue dries, thread a yarn hanger through the carousel roof.

◎ Write about each family member on a separate notecard. Use yarn and tape to attach the card to the corresponding horse.

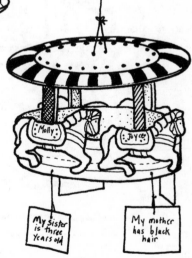

❉ Merry-Go-Round Mobiles ❉

Teaching With Favorite Patricia Polacco Books   Scholastic Professional Books

The Trees of the Dancing Goats

(PENGUIN PUTNAM, 1995)

As Trisha's family prepares to celebrate Hanukkah, they learn that many of their neighbors have been stricken with the fever. Concerned that their friends might not be able to prepare for and celebrate Christmas, the family is moved to action. Working into the night, they prepare food, candles, and small trees decorated with Grandpa's hand-carved toys—goats and other animals lovingly created for his grandchildren for Hanukkah. After delivering the Christmas cheer, the giving family rejoices over the miracle of true friendship as they light the last candles of their Hanukkah celebration.

Related Themes and Topics

▲▲▲▲▲

❋ Family life

❋ Holiday customs

❋ Friendship

❋ Problem-solving

Before Reading

Ask children to think about special celebrations they observe with their families—such as Christmas, Hanukkah, or Kwanzaa—and what they do to prepare for these celebrations. Have them illustrate some of their activities. Then set the drawings aside to use in the After Reading activity. (See page 40.) Introduce the book by telling children that this story is about friends who celebrate the holidays in different ways.

Story Connections

In *The Trees of the Dancing Goats*, the family made latkes. Challenge children to search the following books to find the names and descriptions of other Russian foods: *The Keeping Quilt* (kulich); *Rechenka's Eggs* (kulich and pashka); and *Uncle Vova's Tree* (kutya). Then create and prepare your own simple versions of some of these foods. Check for food allergies before serving the foods.

Tip

▲▲▲▲▲

Other books based on Patricia Polacco's personal and family experiences include *Betty Doll, The Butterfly, Mrs. Mack, Some Birthday!, Thank You, Mr. Falker,* and *Uncle Vova's Tree.* See page 63 for story summaries.

 After Reading

Trisha's family celebrates Hanukkah, while her friends celebrate Christmas. Compare the customs of the two celebrations. How are they alike? Different? Extend the Before Reading activity (see page 39) by having children illustrate two more pages each—one showing their families during the celebration and the other depicting the end of the celebration. Display each child's set of pictures on a large chart labeled "Before," "During," and "After." Ask children to use their picture sequences to tell about their family celebrations.

Dancing-Goat Decorations (Language Arts/Art)

To wish their neighbors well, Trisha's family made sure that a dancing-goat decoration hung on each tree. Invite children to make these dancing goats for family members and friends to whom they want to send holiday wishes. First, have students color and cut out the goat patterns on page 41. Ask them to write holiday wishes and the names of the recipients on the back of their goats, then glue designs cut from gift wrap or designs they make to the front of the goats. Help students attach the legs with brass fasteners, then punch holes to add yarn hangers. Encourage children to present their goat ornaments during the holiday season.

Dancing-Goat Decorations

Happy Holiday Grandma

Dancing-Goat Decorations

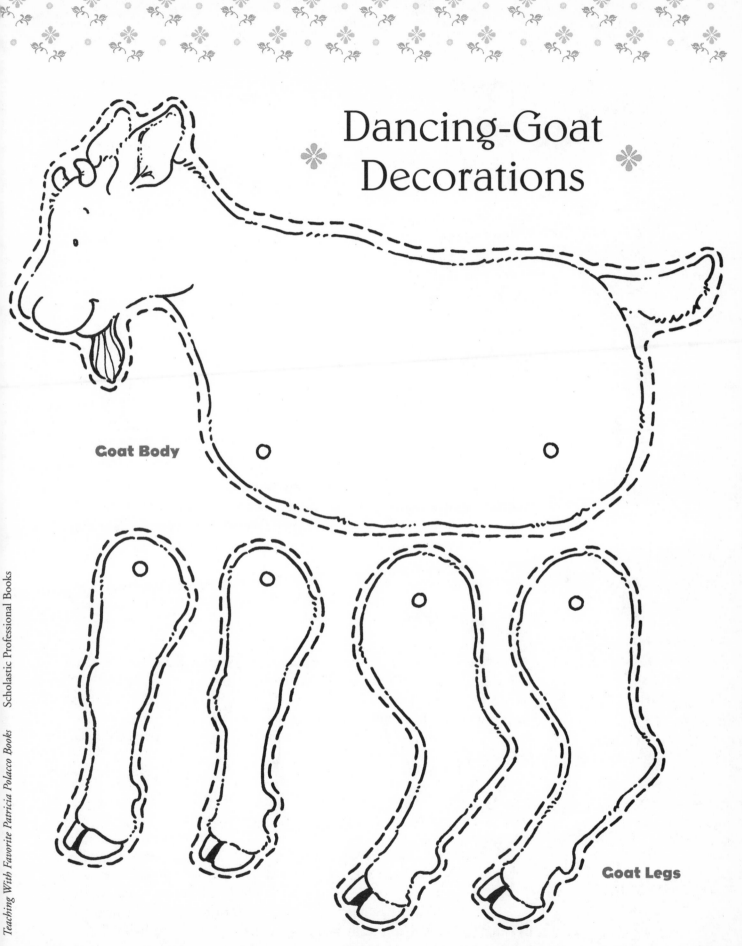

Goat Body

Goat Legs

Meteor!

(PHILOMEL BOOKS, 1987)

Related Themes and Topics

* Country life

* Small-town community

* Meteors/ Falling stars

* Exaggeration

When a meteorite lands smack-dab in the middle of the Gaws' front yard, a quiet little town is struck with meteor madness. In fact, the event turns into quite an extravaganza as townsfolk, schoolchildren, scientists, vendors, dancers, musicians and even a circus visit the mysterious meteorite. And when folks touch that galactic stone, the most extraordinary thing happens—a wonderful kind of magic inspires meteoric experiences!

Before Reading

Show children a fairly large stone. Ask them to examine the stone and share their thoughts about its origins. Then invite students to touch the stone and describe what they feel. (Most likely, children will describe the stone's shape, texture, and possibly temperature—but not their own emotions about the stone.) Afterward, read to your class this story about a special stone that generates feelings of magic and wonder.

After Reading

After reading the story, lead children to understand the rarity of such an event. Invite them to share their thoughts about why the meteorite created so much excitement. Then discuss how the people felt "magic" when they touched the meteorite. Do students think that it really had magical powers? Why or why not?

Writing Wonders (Language Arts)

To inspire some out-of-this-world writing, add this special pencil-holder to your writing center. To make the pencil-holder, cut a large polystyrene ball in half. Paint one half with fluorescent paint to represent a meteorite. After it dries, coat the meteorite with water-thinned craft glue, then sprinkle a thin layer of soil and gold glitter onto the glue. Glue the dry meteorite and a bed of craft grass to sturdy cardboard. Use a pencil to make several holes in the meteorite. Place a sharpened, holographic-design pencil in each hole, and stock your center with copies of the themed writing paper on page 45. With these meteoric pencils and paper, your students' stories are sure to sparkle!

Meteoric Moments (Language Arts)

A lot of meteoric events happened the day after the meteorite landed in Union City! Just as this event stirs up a lot of excitement, so do the accomplishments of your students when they master a skill or reach a goal. Ask children to draw pictures of accomplishments for which they are proud. Have them cut out paper meteorite shapes large enough to fit over their drawings. Invite them to decorate the meteorites with craft materials such as glitter, glitter pens, or splattered fluorescent paint. Have students place their meteorites on top of their drawings, then staple at the top to make a flap. Invite children to share their meteoric accomplishments with the class. Later, display the meteorites with a banner that reads "Meteoric Moments in Our Lives."

Crater Creations (Science)

When the meteorite landed in the Gaws' yard, it created a hole, or crater, in the earth. To understand how a falling object can dent the earth, have children try this simple experiment. Set a shoe box on a spread of newspapers. Mix four cups each of flour and salt in the box. Smooth the mixture with an index card, and then sprinkle the "soil" with ground cinnamon. Invite children to drop one marble (meteorite) at a time onto the soil. (For safety, you might have children wear goggles.) Have them carefully remove each meteorite to observe the resulting crater. Are the craters all the same size? To what do children attribute the different sizes in craters? Encourage children to explore how dropping different-sized marbles from different heights affects crater size.

Tip
▲▲▲▲▲

Explain to students that a meteor is the streak of light seen in the sky when an object enters the atmosphere. Meteorite is the name given to that object when—and if—it lands on earth.

Meteors are also called falling stars. Read *My Rotten Redheaded Older Brother* to discover the wish that Patricia made on a falling star—and its surprising outcome! Then invite children to write or draw wishes for their siblings or friends on star cutouts.

Meteorite Magic (Language Arts)

The townspeople in the story were convinced that the meteorite held a special magic. Create a magical meteorite for your class by painting an egg-sized rock to resemble a glowing meteorite. Then use the meteorite in this game to reinforce basic concepts. To begin, name a letter, color, shape, or category—such as animal, toy, or vehicle. Pass the magic meteorite around the circle of seated children. As children receive the meteorite, encourage them to "use the magic" to help them name something belonging to that category. Have children continue passing the meteorite until everyone has a turn, or until children can't think of any more words. Then name a different category and have the last child start a new round of play.

Exaggeration Station (Language Arts)

The news of the meteorite's landing spread faster than the fire engine could leave the firehouse! And with each retelling, the story grew more and more grandiose in nature. To observe how this might happen, play a round of gossip. Start by passing the meteorite from Meteorite Magic (above) to a child. Then whisper a simple statement to the child. Have him or her add an exaggeration or embellishment to the statement and then whisper it to the next child. Pass the meteorite and the statement around a circle in this manner until both return to you. Then announce the circulated statement to the class. After the giggling subsides, compare it to the original one.

Meteor Math (Math/Movement)

Hit some critical math skills with a beanbag toss game. Cut out nine pieces of green paper, each about one-foot square. Label each with a numeral from 1–9 (or the numeral of your choice). Tape the paper "yards" to the floor in a random arrangement or in the formation of bowling pins. Invite each child to toss three beanbag meteorites onto the yards. According to ability level, have children identify the numeral on each yard their meteorites hit, count aloud to that number, or total the amounts on the yards. For more advanced students, label the yards with simple addition or subtraction facts and have them give the sums of each hit yard.

Name _____ Date _____

✧ Writing Wonders ✧

_____

_____

_____

_____

_____

_____

_____

_____

_____

_____

Teaching With Favorite Patricia Polacco Books   Scholastic Professional Books

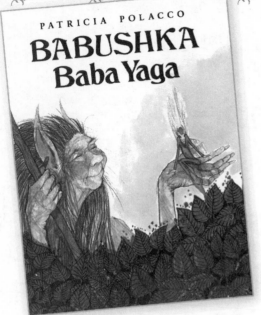

Babushka Baba Yaga

(PENGUIN PUTNAM, 1995)

Disguised as a babushka, Baba Yaga, the legendary woods creature, receives a warm welcome from a young mother, her son, and the people of a small village. But when tales of the horrible Baba Yaga surface, the broken-hearted old woman's fear of being revealed leads her back into the woods—away from her happy life and beloved "grandson." That is, until a crisis reunites them and the villagers discover Baba Yaga's true heart.

Related Themes and Topics

▲▲▲▲▲

❋ Relationships

❋ Feelings

❋ Fear

❋ Conflict resolution

Before Reading

Ask children to name some familiar stories in which a feared creature attempts to befriend a child—such as *Hansel and Gretel* and *Little Red Riding Hood.* Did these creatures (the witch and the wolf, respectively) act out of true concern for the child? After students share their thoughts, tell them that *Babushka Baba Yaga* is a story about an unusual creature that befriends a child. Ask them to listen carefully to determine whether this creature truly cares about the child.

After Reading

Have children discuss whether or not Babushka Baba Yaga truly loved Victor. Then help them label a chart "She Loves Me" and "She Loves Me Not." Under each heading, list the things Baba Yaga did that made Victor feel he was either loved or not loved. Encourage children to discuss their responses and differences of opinions.

Babushka Scarves (Language Arts/Dramatic Play)

Have students examine the colorful clothing in the story. Then guide them in making their own babushka scarves to wear as they retell the story, tell their own babushka stories, or role-play babushkas in the drama center.

◉ Remove the backing from a two-foot-long sheet of clear self-adhesive covering.

◉ Firmly press a sheet of tissue paper to the sticky side of the covering. (Note: wrinkles give the scarf a natural look and tears can be patched with extra tissue.)

◉ Cut the covering into a scarf shape, as shown.

◉ Decorate the tissue side with markers, paint pens, or sponge prints.

◉ Fringe the curved edges and punch holes in the corners.

◉ Affix paper reinforcements over the holes, and then add ribbon ties.

Babushka Boastfest (Language Arts)

In the book, the babushkas gathered and told stories of their grandchildren. To add an interesting twist to such a boastfest, have children gather to share stories of their grandmothers or other adult female friends. Conclude the bragging session by asking children to create written or illustrated tributes to their real or adopted babushkas. If students made the babushka scarves (above), you might display each child's story on a backdrop of his or her scarf.

Tip

▲▲▲▲▲

Students might also use the two sets of babushka cards to play Concentration.

Story Connections

Help children find each Polacco book featuring a babushka. Then have them label a chart with each book title. Ask students to list the characteristics of each babushka under the appropriate title and then compare all of the babushkas. Invite children to describe the traits they would like their own babushkas to have.

Babushka Guessing Game

(Science/Social Studies)

Challenge children's visual discrimination skills with these babushka attribute cards. Copy and identically color two sets of babushka cards (page 49). Cut out the cards and glue each to half of a 3- by 5-inch index card. If desired, laminate the cards for durability. To play, two children each take a set of cards. The first player spreads his or her cards faceup. The second player randomly picks a card from his or her deck, then names an attribute of the babushka on the card, such as "This babushka wears glasses." The second player continues naming attributes until the first child finds the matching card from his or her set. The game continues in this manner until the players have matched up all of the babushka cards. Have players switch roles to play again.

❋ Babushka Guessing Game ❋

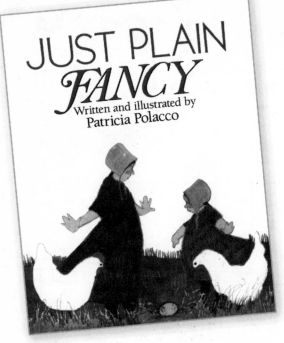

Just Plain Fancy

(PENGUIN PUTNAM, 1995)

Related Themes and Topics

▲▲▲▲▲

❁ Community

❁ Responsibility

❁ Pride in accomplishments

❁ Animal differences

Although the Amish are plain people, Naomi wishes—just once—to have something fancy. And that's just what she gets when she hatches an unusual egg that she found by the roadside. Concerned that she will be shunned for possessing such a fancy creature, Naomi keeps the bird a secret from her family and community. But during her family's frolic, the bird makes a surprise appearance. Even more surprising to Naomi, though, is the response of her people to the beautiful and colorful bird.

Before Reading

Share the following information about the simple Amish lifestyle before sharing *Just Plain Fancy* with students:

◎ The Amish do not own cars, televisions, or radios.

◎ They do not have electric or phone lines connected to their homes.

◎ Telephones are used only when necessary, such as for business or emergencies.

◎ They dress alike because they believe that everyone is equally important.

◎ The Amish work together and take care of each other.

Discussion Starters Ask children to name some of the chores mentioned in the story and the people responsible for them. Then explain that in an Amish community, everybody has specific jobs to do.

To promote community participation in your class, use these "chore" eggs to assign classroom duties. Simply label paper strips with classroom chores. Put each strip into a plastic egg, and then place all of the eggs in a basket. Each morning, have children select and open their eggs to discover the chores for which they will be responsible on that day.

Birds of a Feather (Science)

Conduct this research activity to help children learn about the similarities and differences between chickens and peacocks. First, collect books and other resources about each bird. Divide the class into small groups. Have each group research either the chicken or the peacock. Ask children to prepare posters or models of their bird, as well as written information describing the bird's appearance, egg size, and sounds. Then invite each group to present its findings to the class. Follow up by having the class use what they've learned to compare the characteristics of both birds on chart paper or a Venn diagram.

White Cap Ceremony (Social Studies)

Naomi worked hard to accomplish her goal—to be presented with a white cap. Help children make similar white caps to wear as symbols of their accomplishments. To begin, ask them to gather one end of a 14-inch white tissue-paper square. Have students staple the gathered end, trapping a ribbon tie in the staple. Instruct them to repeat the steps for the other end of their paper squares. Invite a volunteer to stand as you tell about one of his or her accomplishments. After you congratulate the child, tie the cap onto his or her head. (You might also present the child with a certificate of achievement.) Continue the ceremony until you've recognized each child for an accomplishment.

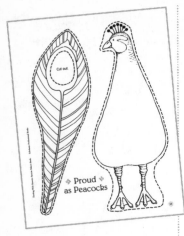

Proud
as Peacocks

Proud as Peacocks (Social Studies)

Students will be as proud as peacocks over this unique display. First, make a copy of page 53 for each child. Ask children to cut out the peacock feather and color it blue and green. Have them cut out the oval and glue a photo or picture of themselves to the back so that it shows through. Next, have them write their names and accomplishments on sentence strips. Color and cut out one enlarged copy of the peacock (page 53). Place the peacock body on a bulletin board, and let children take turns adding their feathers and sentence strips to build the display. Children can cut out additional feathers (leaving the oval intact) and add them to the display if necessary to create a full fan of peacock feathers.

Story
Connections

Patricia Polacco wrote several books featuring birds as significant characters. Discuss with children the roles of the peacock in this story, the goose in *Rechenka's Eggs*, and the wren in *Luba and the Wren*. Invite children to choose one of these birds, or any bird of their choice, to use in real or imaginary stories. Ask them to record and illustrate their stories in booklet form.

Cut out.

❋ Proud ❋
as Peacocks

The Bee Tree
Patricia Polacco

The Bee Tree

(PENGUIN PUTNAM, 1995)

Related Themes and Topics

▲▲▲▲▲

❋ Reading

❋ Friends

❋ Cooperation

❋ Bees

When Mary Ellen tires of reading, her Grampa takes her on a sweet adventure—to find a bee tree. As the two chase one bee "guide" after another, they attract quite a following of friends and neighbors. After collecting honey from the bee tree, all of the friends enjoy the tasty treat together. Grampa uses the honey to illustrate the sweetness of chasing adventure, knowledge, and wisdom through the pages of a book. And Mary Ellen never again tires of reading.

Before Reading

In advance, obtain a recording of Rimsky-Korsakov's "Flight of the Bumblebees." Without identifying the name of the music, play the recording while children listen quietly. When the music stops, ask them to describe what they felt during the song. Did they sense the sound or presence of bees? With the mood set, continue by sharing *The Bee Tree*.

After Reading

Grampa used honey to represent the sweet things—such as knowledge and adventure—that can be chased through books. Explain that children just chased adventure through the pages of *The Bee Tree*. Label a two-column chart "Adventure" and "Knowledge." Ask students to name other books in which they have chased either adventure or knowledge. List their responses under the appropriate headings and discuss what children recall about the various books.

The Bee Tree Game

(Language Arts/Math/Social Skills)

Reinforce various skills with this story-related game. To prepare, color and cut out the game board on pages 56 and 57. Glue the pages together where indicated. Use paint or marker to color several dried lima beans (bees) each a different color. Place a small honey-flavored candy (or another treat) on the tree for each player. Have children form small groups, then follow these steps to play:

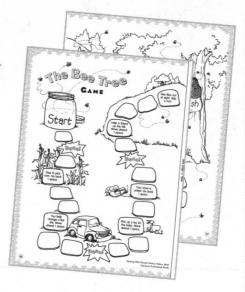

◎ Each player places his or her bee on START. In turn, players toss a penny and move according to how the penny lands: Heads moves two spaces and tails moves one. The player follows any directions on the corresponding space. Players landing on "Buzz!" take another turn.

◎ As each player reaches FINISH, he or she collects a treat.

A Spoonful of Honey (Science/Math)

Perhaps children have tasted a teaspoonful of honey, but do they know that it takes 12 bees to make that amount of honey? Conduct this experiment to help students determine how many bees it takes to produce different quantities of honey. To set up, sequence a set of measuring cups on a table. Have children fill each cup with one teaspoon of water at a time until the cup is full. As one child fills the cup, have another use tally marks to keep track of the number of spoonfuls. After the cups are full, count the tally marks and multiply by twelve. The result is the number of bees required to produce that quantity of honey!

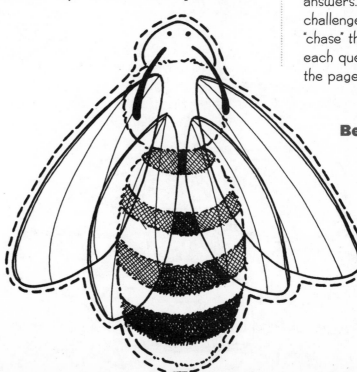

In both *The Bee Tree* and *Thank You, Mr. Falker*, Polacco refers to the sweetness of knowledge and how it can be "chased through the pages of a book." To help children chase knowledge through a book, enlarge, copy and cut out a supply of the bee pattern below. On the back of the bees, write questions related to a book of your choice. Include page references on which children can find answers. Then challenge students to "chase" the answers to each question through the pages of the book.

Bee Pattern

The Bee Tree
GAME

Start

Bee flies out of sight. Skip a turn.

Help a friend up the hill. Move ahead 1 space.

Buzz!

Buzz!

Stop to pick corn. Go back 1 space.

Your shoe is untied. Go back 1 space.

You help change a flat tire. Move ahead 1 space.

Pick up a toy for the baby. Move ahead 1 space.

Buzz!

Teaching With Favorite Patricia Polacco Books
Scholastic Professional Books

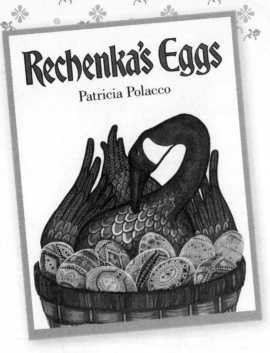

Rechenka's Eggs

(PENGUIN PUTNAM, 1995)

Related Themes and Topics

▲▲▲▲▲▲

❋ Compassion

❋ Friendship

❋ Giving

Every year, Babushka's hand-painted eggs win first place at the Easter Festival in Moskva. But this year there's no reason to go to the festival, for her beautifully decorated eggs are accidentally broken by Rechenka, an injured goose that Babushka nurses back to health. Then a miracle happens! Rechenka lays a brilliantly colored egg each day until Babushka's shattered eggs are replaced. And while Babushka takes first place once again at the Festival, Rechenka leaves one final and memorable gift before returning to the wild.

Before Reading

Animals can become injured in many different ways. Ask children to share their experiences with (or stories about) injured animals—perhaps a cat with a sore foot or a bird with a broken wing. Did someone take care of the animal until the injury healed? What happened to the animal after it got well? After your discussion, introduce the story by telling students that *Rechenka's Eggs* is a story about a woman who helped an injured animal.

After Reading

Even after Rechenka broke Babushka's eggs, the old woman continued to be kind to the goose. Discuss the ways in which Babushka extended kindness to Rechenka. Then recall how the goose repaid Babushka. Let children label egg cutouts with ways in which they have shown kindness to others. Display the eggs in a large basket cutout with the title "A Basket Full of Kindness."

Hatching Geese (Art/Science)

Review the illustrations of the hatching goose, and then invite children to make their own hatching geese following the directions below. To learn more about the egg-hatching process, share *Anca Hariton's Egg Story* (Dutton Children's Books, 1992) or *Egg: A Photographic Story of Hatching* by Robert Burton (Dorling Kindersley, 2000). Encourage students to use their eggs to describe the hatching process.

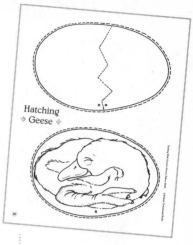

Hatching
Geese

◎ Color and cut out the eggs on page 60.

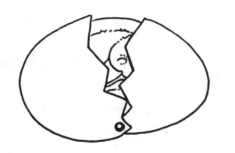

◎ Cut the egg without the goose in two pieces.

◎ Use a brass fastener to attach the two egg parts to the whole egg, so that the pieces open and close to conceal and reveal the baby goose.

Eggs in the Balance (Science/Math)

Instead of using whole eggs, Babushka painted hollow eggs for the festival. Invite children to compare the weight of an empty shell to a whole egg with this experiment. To begin, make a small hole at both ends of an egg, then blow the contents of the egg into a bowl. (Teacher only. Make sure to wash your hands after handling the raw egg.) Rinse the egg, then place it in a clear plastic tumbler. Place a whole egg in another tumbler. Set an empty tumbler on one side of a scale and provide a supply of pennies. Ask children to place one of the egg-filled tumblers on the scale opposite the empty tumbler. Have them add one penny at a time to the empty tumbler until the scale balances. Ask students to count the penny weights and record the number, and then repeat the activity with the other egg-filled tumbler. Which egg weighs more? Why?

✦ Story ✦
Connections

Babushka painted her eggs, but the children in *Chicken Sunday* created wax designs on their eggs and then dipped them in dye. Regardless of the technique, all the eggs turned out beautiful! Let children cut out eggs from paper plates. Have them paint designs on the eggs, or use crayons to draw designs on the eggs, and then brush them with watercolor paints. (To simplify the process, you can have children dip the crayon-design eggs in a tray of food-colored water. The area coated with crayon will resist the color to bring out students' designs.)

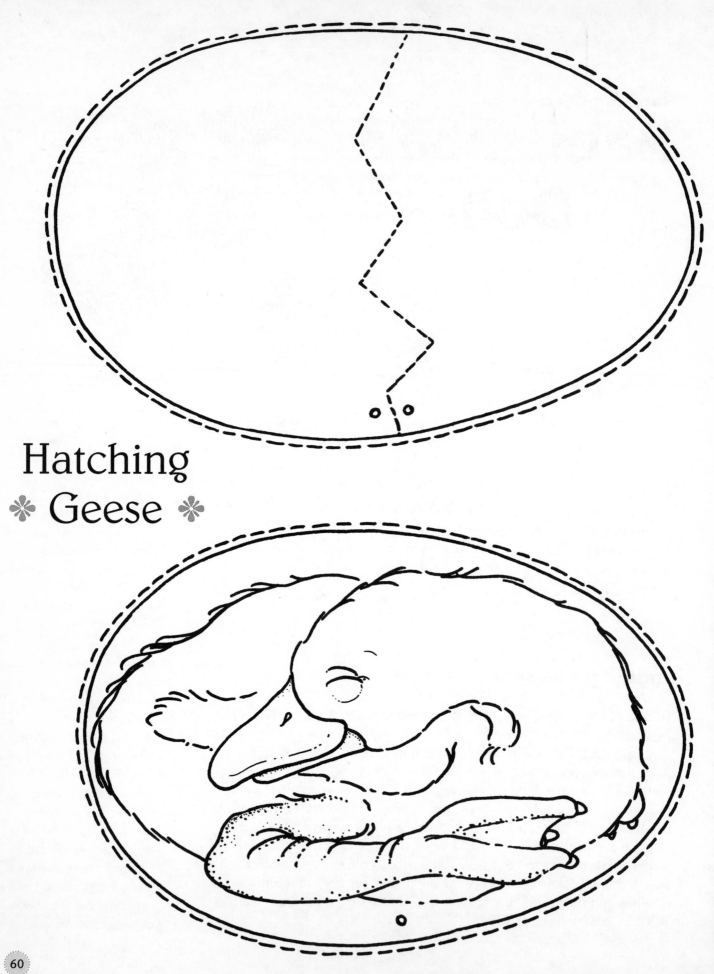

Hatching
❋ Geese ❋

Teaching With Favorite Patricia Polacco Books

Scholastic Professional Books

Babushka's Doll

(PENGUIN PUTNAM BOOKS FOR
YOUNG READERS, 1995)

Impatient Natasha constantly demands time and attention, preventing Babushka from completing her chores. So to keep her granddaughter busy while she goes for groceries, Babushka encourages Natasha to play with a special doll. Much to Natasha's surprise, the doll comes to life and immediately begins making demands on the little girl. Finally, tired and frustrated, Natasha wishes for the doll to be just a doll again. And Babushka returns to find that Natasha is quite a nice little girl after all.

Related Themes and Topics

▲▲▲▲▲

❋ Family life

❋ Patience

❋ Conflict resolution

Before Reading

Have students ever had a favorite doll or stuffed animal? After sharing experiences, show students *Babushka's Doll*. Ask them to listen to the story to find out why this doll is so special.

After Reading

Natasha was totally surprised when the doll came to life, especially when it began to make such demands on her! Discuss with children how Natasha must have felt about the "live" doll. Then encourage them to imagine that one of their dolls or stuffed animals has suddenly come to life. Have them write about and illustrate their imaginary experiences and feelings. Afterward, invite students to share their stories with the class.

Patricia Polacco features babushkas in a number of stories. Have children recall any variations of the name Babushka. Then have them look at the dedication in *Babushka's Mother Goose* to discover additional references to "Babushka."

Tip
▲▲▲▲▲

Other books based on the fiction, fantasy, and folktales of Patricia Polacco include *Appelemando's Dreams, I Can Hear the Sun, In Enzo's Splendid Gardens, Luba and the Wren, Mrs. Katz and Tush,* and *Tivkah Means Hope.* See page 63 for story summaries.

Wishing Doll (Language Arts)

Natasha's wish for the doll to be "just a doll again" came true in the story. Invite children to make school-related wishes with this special doll.

 Wrap a tissue box in sparkly gift paper, cutting the paper away from the top opening. Label the box "Dear Wishing Doll."

 Display a large cloth doll with the box. To use, have students label notecards with "I wish…," finish the sentence with a school-related wish, and then drop their notecards into the box. At the end of the day, select a few cards from the box and read the wishes to the class. Discuss how each wish might be granted, or may have already come true.

More Books by Patricia Polacco

◉ **Appelemando's Dreams** (Philomel, 1991). Appelemando and his friends get lost and realize that their only hope of rescue lies in a dream.

◉ **Aunt Chip and the Great Triple Creek Dam Affair** (Philomel, 1996). Aunt Chip helps a TV-crazed town discover the true treasures of books.

◉ **Betty Doll** (Penguin, 2001). Mary Ellen shares her feelings and life experiences with Betty Doll, a doll lovingly made from scraps of cloth.

◉ **The Butterfly** (Philomel, 2000). Sevrine develops a secret friendship with a Jewish girl whose family is hiding in the cellar.

◉ **I Can Hear the Sun** (Philomel, 1996). The orphan Fondo finds a friend who is like him in many ways—and who also believes in him.

◉ **In Enzo's Splendid Gardens** (Philomel, 1997). A boy's fascination with a bee inadvertently sets off a whimsical chain of events.

◉ **Luba and the Wren** (Philomel, 1999). Kind-hearted Luba rescues a wren that grants her any wish. Content with her life, Luba has no wish—but her parents do!

◉ **Mrs. Katz and Tush** (Bantam, 1992). Larnel shares the care of a kitten and a unique friendship with the widowed Mrs. Katz.

◉ **Mrs. Mack** (Philomel, 1998). Patricia finally realizes her lifelong dream—to learn to ride a horse! But she learns more than just riding skills from her instructor.

◉ **Some Birthday!** (Simon & Schuster, 1991). When Patricia goes to the Clay Pit with Dad, she experiences an exciting, spooky birthday surprise.

◉ **Thank You, Mr. Falker** (Philomel, 1998). Trisha's enthusiasm for school slowly dies, until compassionate Mr. Falker helps her discover the magic of reading.

◉ **Tivkah Means Hope** (Doubleday, 1994). A firestorm engulfs the Roths' neighborhood—and Tivkah the cat disappears.

◉ **Uncle Vova's Tree** (Philomel, 1989). Christmas at Uncle Vova's means aromatic scents, magical laughter, lively dancing, and a special tree tradition.

Story Connections

Patricia Polacco once had a very special cat named Tush. This beloved pet inspired the author to write *Mrs. Katz and Tush*. Invite children to share stories about special pets in their lives.

Also by Patricia Polacco

▲▲▲▲▲

❋ *Babushka's Mother Goose* (Philomel, 1995)

❋ *Boatride With Lillian Two Blossom* (Philomel, 1988)

❋ *Picnic at Mudsock Meadow* (Putnam, 1992)

Author Study Celebration

Use this collection of ideas to conclude your Patricia Polacco author study and celebrate children's learning.

◎ Have children vote for their favorite Polacco books. Graph and compare the results.

◎ Invite children to dress as a character from one of the books. Have children, one at a time, model their characters down a "runway" and then share some information about the characters.

◎ Have several groups create promotional posters about Patricia Polacco and her books. Display the posters in the library or hallways.

◎ Remind students that Polacco's stories are often inspired by memorable moments in her life. Ask children to share the most memorable moments or events of their school year and what made these times special. Don't be surprised if some of the special memories are related to your Patricia Polacco author study!

◎ Invite children to create a mask in the style of a Patricia Polacco character to retell a story. A paper plate makes a simple mask framework. Have students cut out holes for eyes, then trim the plate so that it ends below the nose. Students can then customize the plate to create their mask, adding features such as hair and earrings or a hat. Have students attach a wide craft-stick handle to complete the mask.

◎ Pull out the rocking chair and invite volunteers to read Polacco's stories to small groups. Children might also share their own Polacco-inspired tales.

◎ Write individual and class letters to Patricia Polacco. Include photos of related class projects with the letters. Or contact the author via her Web site.

◎ Gather a supply of commercially prepared tape recordings of Polacco's books, or ask parent volunteers to record some of her stories. Keep your listening center stocked with these tapes and the corresponding books so that children can enjoy the stories, even after your author study is completed.